D1389394

04297055

ICONS
OF
STYLE

T-SHIRTS

MITCHELL BEAZLEY

T-SHIRTS

The
DAILY
STREET

Contents

6 The T-shirt is an incredibly versatile piece of clothing that is worn by men and women of all ages, all over the world. For many they are basic everyday items, but for some they represent much more, something both covetable and collectable.

Most of the content of this book concerns graphic T-shirts, particularly those from the realms of skate- and streetwear. Streetwear is particularly fond of the T-shirt – they are an effective way for consumers to show what they're into, who they support and what they're all about, and the relatively low cost means that they can be consumed regularly without blowing the bank. For brands, the T-shirt is the perfect platform to convey their particular message, whether their intention is to increase publicity and spark reactions or simply to access new customers with unique and interesting designs.

One particularly special element of streetwear design is its tendency to re-appropriate imagery from popular culture and twist it to make something new. In fact, many of the symbols that are integral to some of streetwear's biggest names are based on the branding of other companies or have borrowed heavily from other inspirations. This made creating this book particularly challenging as we were unable to feature some of our favourite designs and indeed some of the most recognized streetwear T-shirts. Some brands quite simply did not hold the rights to grant permission to use their designs and in some cases had already been involved in legal disputes over the use of copyrighted imagery.

Introduction

This book focuses on the most revered designs from skateboarding and streetwear history. Some of the oldest designs are still in regular use today and remain some of the most popular, while others are produced in strictly limited numbers, selling out almost instantly and available only to the luckiest customers.

The story begins with the T-shirt's military origins and how this style was eventually adopted into popular culture. Long before streetwear was a common term, there was skateboarding, and many of today's biggest brands owe a lot to names like Powell Peralta, Vision and Santa Cruz, which established an interest in graphic design and illustration through skateboards and created an appetite for these on T-shirts in the years that followed.

Streetwear began to come into its own in the early 1990s with brands such as X-Large, Fuct and SSUR, which blended skateboarding's history with hip-hop styling, an artistic understanding and, crucially, a knowledge of branding and design. These names set the standard to which most modern brands still aspire and established many of the fundamental ingredients of streetwear today.

In streetwear's modern age trends come and go, disappearing as quickly as they arrive, but even the last few years have produced designs that will no doubt go on to be the icons of future generations. This list of 50 of the most iconic T-shirt designs goes some way to exploring the journey that the T-shirt has undergone over the last hundred or so years and highlights some of the great stories that have helped keep things interesting along the way.

White T-shirt

1898

There seems no better place to begin than with the humble white T-shirt – without doubt the most iconic T-shirt of all. From its first appearance in the 1800s to its importance as a fashion staple in the modern day, the simple white T-shirt is an unrivalled classic.

The garment we now know as the T-shirt has military origins, first issued to US naval personnel around the time of the Spanish–American War in 1898 and intended purely as underwear to be worn beneath the uniform. It got its name from the 'T'-shaped appearance formed by the body and short sleeves and was usually made from an inexpensive cotton that made it both lightweight and easy to clean.

Soon after, the T-shirt was adopted by the US Army and given to all recruits as part of their standard uniform. Veterans and off-duty soldiers began wearing the T-shirt as casual clothing, which took the garment outside of its military confines for the first time and brought it to an entirely new audience.

In the 1951 film *A Streetcar Named Desire*, Marlon Brando wore a fitted white T-shirt throughout much of the film (it could also be seen on the movie's promotional posters). This would help popularize the T-shirt as outerwear, with many men of the time hoping to emulate Brando's signature look, and the T-shirt has remained a wardrobe essential ever since.

The plain white T-shirt is incredibly versatile and is at home in almost every style and subculture. When it comes to streetwear, many of the T-shirts in this book are built on the foundations of the classic white T-shirt, the simplicity of which has helped give these designs iconic status.

Opposite: The T-shirt was first issued to US naval personnel around the time of the Spanish–American War in 1898 and is seen here in 1918.

The Trefoil logo has been in regular use by adidas since 1972 and could be found on almost all adidas products until the mid-1990s. Adolf 'Adi' Dassler began producing sports footwear in the 1920s with the intention of creating the best possible footwear for athletes, and the brand has grown to be one of the world's biggest manufacturers of sports footwear, clothing and accessories.

The Trefoil is a flower-like design that incorporates the brand's three-stripe motif through the centre and features the company name underneath. Through its transformation of the three stripes into three leaves, the logo represented a new age for adidas and helped to signify the brand's growing diversity. In the mid-1990s adidas switched its main branding to a triangular version of the original three-stripe motif. Today the Trefoil symbolizes adidas's rich heritage and is the main logo of the adidas Originals brand.

The Trefoil T-shirt is just one of many products that have featured the Trefoil logo over the years. It is an internationally recognized symbol and now resonates outside of its original sportswear confines, becoming popular among fashion consumers. It is normally found printed centred across the chest accompanied by the adidas name underneath (the typeface used is a custom type developed for and owned by adidas) and sometimes also features the Originals brand name below.

Opposite: The Trefoil was adidas's primary logo from 1972 until it was replaced in the mid-1990s.

11

adidas
Trefoil logo

1972

Vision Street Wear was founded in 1976 by Brad Dorfman as a clothing, footwear and skateboard brand. Dorfman and Vision Street Wear are credited as responsible for taking skateboard clothing outside of simple printed T-shirts and sweatshirts with an extended range of more fashionable apparel, something that is now commonplace for most modern skateboard brands.

Vision launched at just the right time, capitalizing on the late 1970s boom in skateboarding following the arrival of polyurethane wheels and the opening of the first public skateparks. Vision was known for its bold, colourful graphics and many of the company's products were printed with the now-iconic Vision Street Wear Box logo. The design featured the three words of the company name stacked on top of one another encased within a square box. The first word was usually red, with the 'wear' portion of the name surrounded by a smaller, rectangular box. The design appeared like a stamp of approval on Vision Street Wear products and packaging and became an internationally recognized symbol.

Dorfman eventually sold the licence to the Vision Street Wear name, and the branding has been used by a number of other companies since its original issue. It now serves as a nostalgic reminder of early skateboard design and remains popular the world over.

Opposite: The Box logo was like a stamp of approval on Vision Street Wear products and packaging.

13

Vision Street Wear Box logo

1976

Independent Truck Company logo

Established in 1978, the Independent Truck Company is one of the oldest and most successful skateboard companies in existence. Founded by business partners Richard Novak, Jay Shiurman, Fausto Vitello and Eric Swenson, the company set out to create a quality skateboard truck for an expanding skateboard market that would do a better job than the other options available at the time.

The Independent logo seen today has been in place since the very beginning and was inspired by the Alisee Cross (a version of the Iron Cross with curved edges) as worn on the vestment of Pope John Paul II, which was spotted in a copy of *Time* magazine. The cross contains the Independent name through its centre with Truck Company text underneath and is usually presented in a combination of black, white and red.

The company's reputation for providing the best product available means that Independent trucks are still used by many skateboard pros, with the brand's huge team regularly sporting Independent branded apparel, which serves as a great marketing tool. Like many other skateboard brands of the era, Independent's logo designs now also have a following outside of the skateboarding world. The brand's collaboration with Supreme in 2012 and a collection of footwear and clothing with Vans in 2014 have helped extend Independent's appeal outside of skateboarding in recent years.

Opposite: The Independent logo seen today has been in place since the very beginning and was inspired by the Alisee Cross.

Powell Peralta
'Ripper'

1978

Powell Peralta's 'Ripper' is one of skateboarding's most recognizable designs from one of the oldest skateboard brands. The company was founded in 1978 by George Powell and Stacy Peralta, and in 1979 they formed the now infamous Bones Brigade skate team, made up of skateboarding legends Tony Hawk, Rodney Mullen, Steve Caballero, Mike McGill, Tommy Guerrero and Lance Mountain.

Powell Peralta was known for having some of the best board graphics in skateboarding, bringing elements of punk and heavy-metal imagery into its designs. One of the best examples is the 'Ripper' graphic, which features a skeletal figure bursting through the board and peeling back the artwork around it. The 'Ripper' was designed by artist Vernon Courtland Johnson who was responsible for many of the best-selling Powell Peralta graphics and would prove to be a huge inspiration to many in the years that followed.

As well as skateboards, the 'Ripper' graphic regularly appeared on T-shirts, sometimes accompanied by the Powell name but now more commonly seen with Bones text behind the image in the same typeface, the logo now used by Powell subsidiary Bones Bearings. In 2009 Powell celebrated the legacy created by Vernon Courtland Johnson's artwork with the Rip the Ripper Art Show in which 58 artists each created their own take on the 'Ripper' design, honouring 30 years since its first release.

Opposite: The 'Ripper' was designed by artist Vernon Courtland Johnson who was responsible for much of the imagery in the Powell Peralta graphics.

Stüssy
Basic logo

Beginning life on the beaches of early 1980s California, Stüssy is known as the forefather of all that is modern streetwear. The brand still holds a considerable presence more than 30 years later and today remains one of the most popular. Many of Stüssy's modern T-shirts are based around a series of designs crafted in its earliest days, including the basic script logo. Most often found printed large across the chest or shoulders of black or white T-shirts, the Basic logo is based on the hand-drawn script of the brand's founder, Shawn Stüssy.

Starting his own surfboard company at the age of 24, Shawn would sign his work with his surname in thick black marker, basing his own signature on that of his artist uncle, Jan Stüssy. Shawn began experimenting with clothing as a means of promoting his surfboards, screen-printing his signature across the chest and unintentionally giving birth to a now-legendary brand and streetwear powerhouse.

This signature logo can be found on many of Stüssy's products, its promotional materials and indeed its storefronts in locations all over the world. The fact that such a logo is still the basis for some of the brand's biggest-selling pieces of clothing decades later speaks volumes about the importance of good design and what a great logo can do for a brand.

Opposite:
Stüssy's Basic logo is based on the hand-drawn signature of the brand's founder, Shawn Stüssy.

With its Link logo, Stüssy took one of the most iconic logos in fashion and made it their own, creating a powerful icon for the brand in the process. Taking the identity of Chanel's interlocking 'C's, the Link logo places two 'S's back to back in the same style, surrounded by the same thin circle.

Chanel's logo of interlocking 'C's is one of the greatest pieces of branding ever created. It's about as simple as they come, but powerful beyond definition. It is also one of the most parodied, with skate and streetwear brands like Palace and SSUR also releasing their own interpretations.

Stüssy's line has long been influenced by high fashion and this homage sums up that connection nicely. Stüssy even continued the story with another T-shirt design based on the Chanel No. 5 label and with nods to Versace and Louis Vuitton in other designs. These examples were the foundation for all of the pop-culture appropriation and popular references that would become a fundamental part of streetwear. Brands like Fuct and Supreme would carry this torch through the 1990s, for it to be taken on by the likes of The Hundreds, HUF and Crooks & Castles in the years that followed. All of these brands owe a great deal to Stüssy, as do most of the names in this book.

Stüssy
Link logo

1980

Thrasher
magazine logo

1981

Thrasher is one of the world's biggest skateboarding magazines, but today it is known for its clothing almost as much as for its editorial content. The magazine was founded in California in 1981 by the trio of Eric Swenson, Kevin Thatcher and Fausto Vitello, two of whom were responsible for starting the Independent Truck Company (see pages 14–15) three years prior. *Thrasher* helped bring skateboarding to the masses, but also kept kids up to date on the latest products from skateboard brands, so was an important tool for the promotion of skateboard clothing.

The magazine logo T-shirt features the classic version of the *Thrasher* logo from the print magazine (an arched form of the Banco typeface) printed across the chest, accompanied by the words 'skateboard magazine' below. Today it is one of the most popular T-shirts in skateboarding and is worn by the most dedicated skaters as well as those with only a casual interest, having been picked up by the fashion consumer in recent years.

Several variations of the design have also appeared as part of some of *Thrasher*'s collaboration products, including a 2011 collaboration with Supreme and projects with HUF in 2013 and 2014. These have helped grow *Thrasher*'s appeal outside of its skateboarding roots.

Opposite and following pages: These T-shirts feature the classic version of the *Thrasher* logo from the long-standing print magazine.

Spitfire
Bighead logo

1987

Spitfire is one of the most widely available and popular skateboard wheel companies, available in most skate shops across the world. Founded in 1987, the brand is part of San Francisco-based Deluxe Distribution, which distributes respected truck companies Thunder and Venture along with brands Anti Hero, Real and Krooked Skateboards.

The Spitfire mascot is a flame-headed character named Bighead, with a menacing grin, designed for the brand by artist Kevin Ancell. The logo appears regularly across Spitfire's extensive range of skateboard wheels, but also throughout the brand's collection of clothing and accessories. The bold cartoon imagery makes Spitfire product easily identifiable and has helped the brand's clothing products, particularly T-shirts, become popular among younger skateboarders.

The Bighead logo can be found in various colours and styles, most commonly printed large on the chest of T-shirts and sweatshirts. The design often undergoes radical transformations, with past variations including a dripping zombie design in several colours and a popular Stars and Stripes-filled version called Flaghead, and has also featured on several footwear models produced in collaboration with Vans. The Spitfire team includes pros Andrew Reynolds, Peter Ramondetta and Dennis Busenitz among many others, who help to market the designs while touring across the world.

Opposite: The Spitfire mascot is a flame-headed character named Bighead, designed by Kevin Ancell.

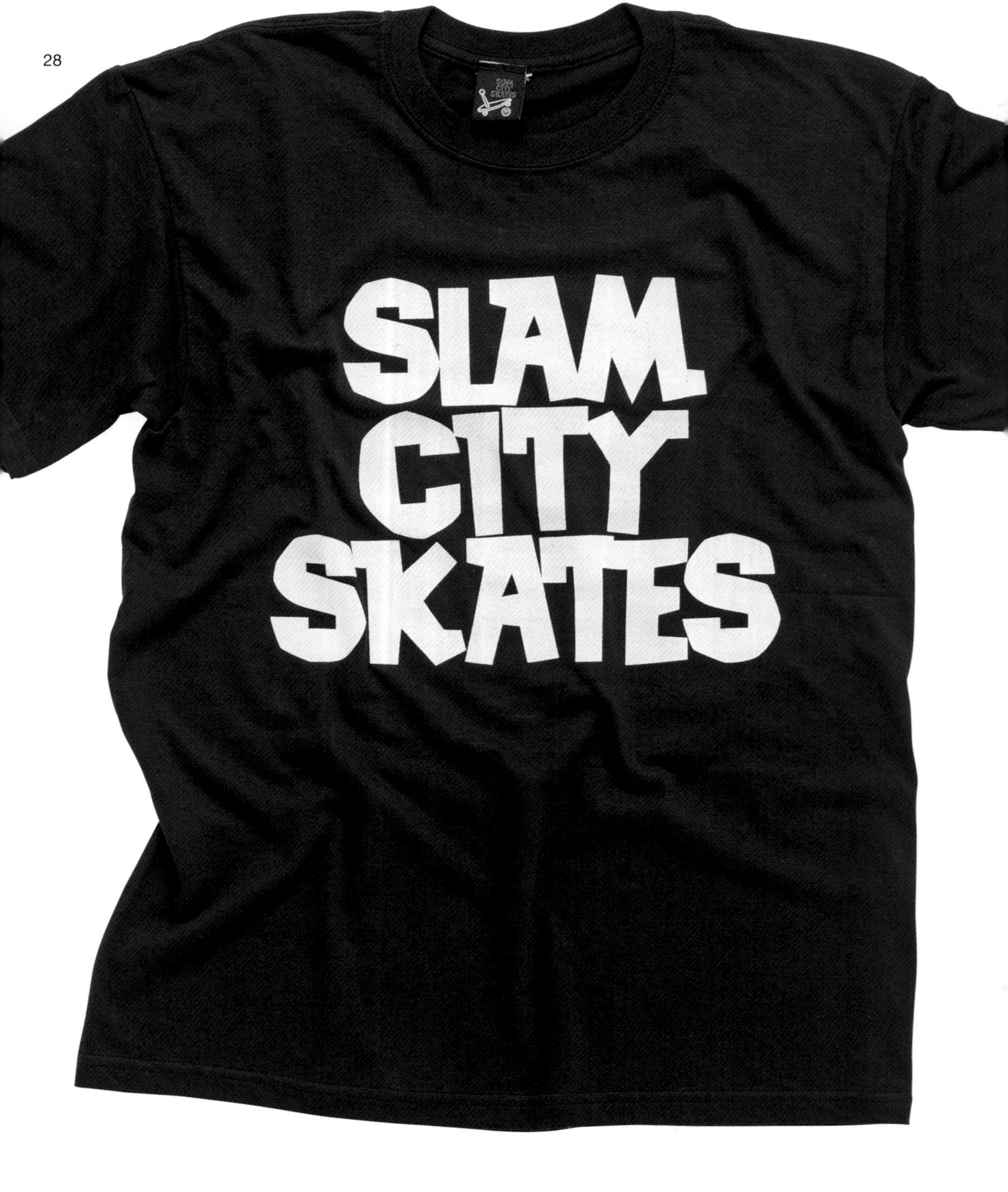
SLAM
CITY
SKATES

Slam City Skates has been a bastion of London skateboarding since the store first opened in Covent Garden in 1988. The idea was born from the mind of skateboarder Paul Sunman in 1986 while working at the now-legendary Rough Trade Records. Paul recognized the lack of availability of skateboards in London and set about fixing that, eventually opening the first Slam store two years later. Slam became the go-to spot for skateboard hardware in London, and while many others have come and gone, it remains a mainstay of British skateboarding decades later.

The store still maintains much of its original character, like the Phil Frost artwork surrounding the exterior walls and, on the ceiling of the basement level, the signatures of the many skateboard greats who have passed through. Slam expanded to a second location in East London in 2013, but the original Covent Garden shop is still high on the itinerary for anyone visiting London with an interest in skateboarding. The Slam City Skates logo T-shirt has become an essential purchase for visiting customers as well as local skateboarders who have been supporting the store throughout its history. Featuring the store's name in a large text placement across the chest, often finished with the 'London' stamp underneath, the design has become a recognized symbol of skateboard culture internationally and undoubtedly one of the most popular shop T-shirts of all time.

Opposite:
The Slam City
Skates logo
has become an
internationally
recognized
symbol of
skateboard
culture.

29

Slam City Skates logo

1988

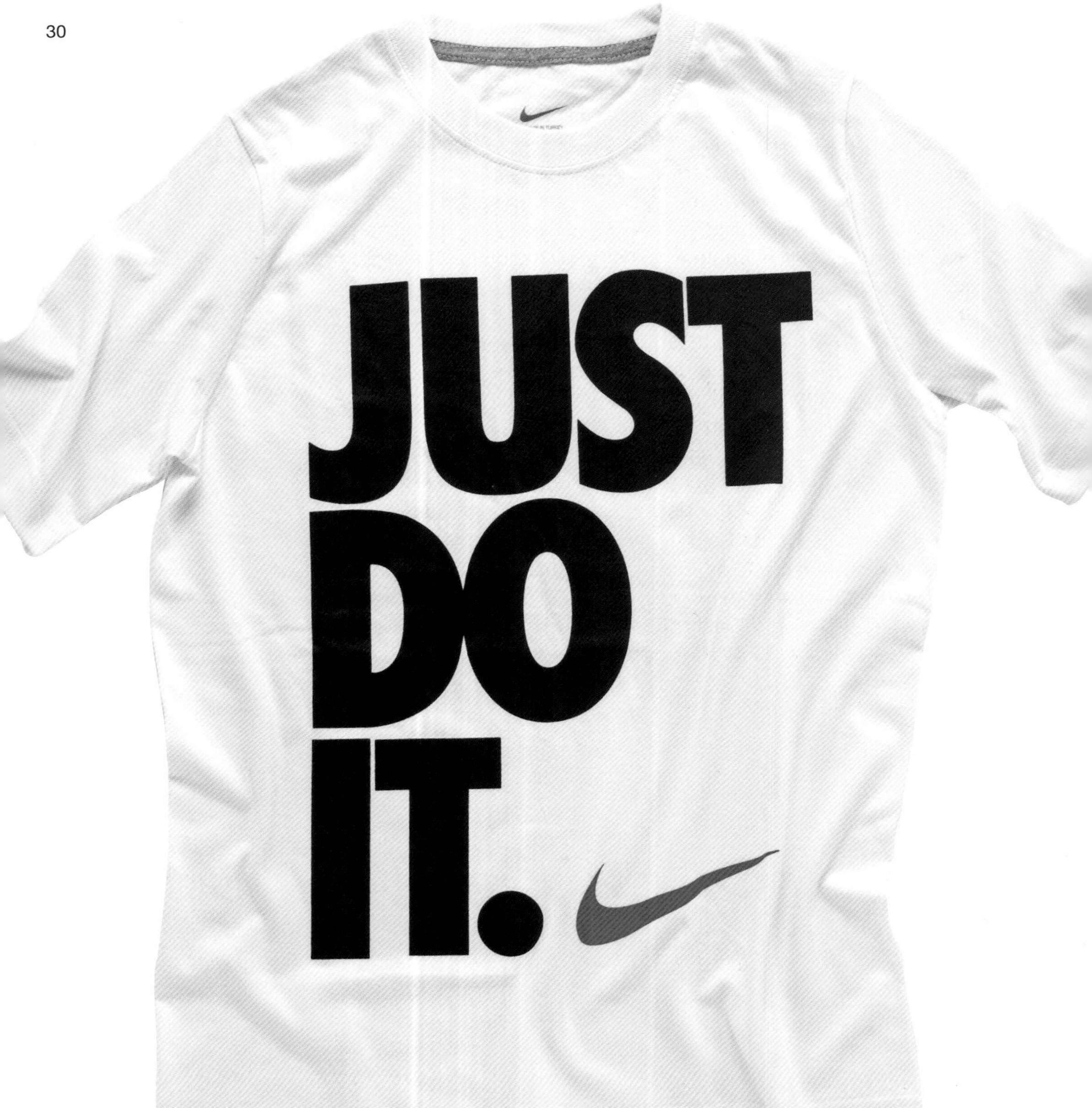
JUST
DO
IT.

Nike's 'Just Do It.' campaign was a hugely successful vehicle for the sports brand when the campaign launched in 1988. The slogan dreamed up in an advertising meeting by the brains at Wieden+Kennedy spoke volumes – a simple phrase that encapsulated the brand and offered a call to action for all those who would see it in the years to come.

Nike is well known for its powerful and inspiring advertising campaigns, but the 'Just Do It.' story broke out of print adverts and billboards into a whole world of merchandise. The large, bold text added weight to the already powerful statement, finished with a full stop to signify the end of all discussion – no ifs, no buts, just do it. Today, the 'Just Do It.' slogan can still be purchased on a select range of sportswear products and accessories.

The typeface used is Futura Condensed Extra Bold, a commercial typeface regularly used throughout Nike's branding but also in common use in many other places. T-shirts usually featured the enlarged text covering almost all of the chest area, and classic versions of the design came complete with an angled red box containing the Nike name and Swoosh, though these is usually replaced with just the Swoosh on modern versions. Now that the slogan is no longer in frequent use, Nike's 'Just Do It.' product offers a certain amount of nostalgia for those who experienced it almost everywhere they went throughout the 1990s.

Opposite: Nike's 'Just Do It.' story moved from print adverts and billboards into a wide range of merchandise.

Nike
'Just Do It.'

1988

Stüssy
'World Tour'

1989

Another hugely popular design from Stüssy is the combination of some of the key logos that have formed part of Stüssy's collections for years. Mixing both the original signature of the brand's founder, Shawn Stüssy (see pages 18–19), and the appropriated Link logo (see pages 20–1), the 'World Tour' design showcases another element of the Stüssy brand that has been a huge part of building its legacy – the International Stüssy Tribe.

Designed to resemble the merchandise made by bands and musicians touring the world, the 'World Tour' T-shirt certifies Stüssy's place as a truly global brand and its importance both as a fashion label and a streetwear staple. Instead of tour dates and performance locations, the 'World Tour' design displays locations key to Stüssy's global domination, where the brand's influential family of 'tribe members' were located. The front lists the fashion capitals of the world – New York, Los Angeles, Tokyo, London and Paris – while the back lists locations of a different kind, those that are key to Stüssy's surf and streetwear roots.

Highlighting areas like Santa Ana and Venice, Brooklyn and the Bronx, alongside illustrious locations like London and Paris, is a great juxtaposition and one that goes some way to illustrating the range of the brand's appeal. The typography used on both sides further emphasizes the contrast by playing tight, neat lettering off against hand-drawn script.

Importantly, these are all locations that have been hugely important to building the Stüssy brand for different reasons. Los Angeles, New York and Tokyo are now also home to Stüssy flagship stores.

Opposite: Instead of tour dates and performance locations, the 'World Tour' design displays locations key to Stüssy's global domination.

A collection of
some of Stüssy's
most successful
designs including
the Basic logo,
'World Tour' and
Link logo T-shirts

35

SSUR
'Signature'

SSUR is a streetwear legend and truly deserves its place among the most iconic labels. Founded in the late 1980s by artist Russ Karablin in New York, SSUR's designs brought with them a political flavour, referencing taboo subjects and not afraid to spark a little controversy. The brand name is its founder's name backwards, the idea for which originated from the way Russ would sign his signature in reverse on each of his paintings, and also a nod to his Russian heritage. Like Fuct, X-Large and other brands of this particular period, SSUR would go on to have a huge influence on streetwear as a whole and all of the brands that followed in their wake.

Much of the SSUR collection sports a dark and moody black-and-white colour palette, with many of the pieces finished with Russ's signature in red on the sleeve, as if he were signing off another of his artworks. This logo has become an integral part of SSUR's branding and features here printed across the chest of the 'Signature' T-shirt in the brand's trademark red.

The SSUR name has evolved to house a number of brands under its umbrella, including Caviar Cartel and The Cut labels, and there are SSUR flagship stores in New York, Los Angeles, Shanghai and Odessa.

Opposite: SSUR's 'Signature' T-shirt features the graffiti-style signature of the brand's founder, artist Russ Karablin.

37

We have mentioned a few times streetwear's tendency to appropriate and adapt the iconography of more recognized brands, but this logo-flip from Erik Brunetti's Fuct was to become one of the most iconic examples. Taking the blue oval badge of the Ford Motor Company, keeping the white script intact but tweaking the lettering to read 'Fuct', was a bold statement and exactly the sort of controversial message that Brunetti wanted to convey when launching the brand during the financial turbulence of 1990.

Following its release, the 'Ford Logo' T-shirt began to pop up in all kinds of places, including an appearance in the music video for Rage Against the Machine's 'Bullet in the Head', on the chest of front man Zack de la Rocha. The design, of course, wasn't taken too kindly by those at the source of its inspiration but, unlike many of the more controversial streetwear T-shirts, Fuct seemed to get away with this parody. Having appeared in various colours since its original release, the design lives on as the brand's most iconic T-shirt graphic.

Even those unfamiliar with the Fuct brand or even streetwear as a whole may recognize this particular design, as it was quickly picked up by bootleggers and can be found on market stalls all over the world.

Opposite: The 'Ford Logo' design from Fuct has become one of the most iconic examples of streetwear's appropriation of recognizable symbols.

Fuct
'Ford Logo'

1990

X-Large
OG logo

1991

X-Large is a true originator of the streetwear image and is known for its influence on style. Opening in Los Angeles in 1991, the first X-Large store was the epicentre of an erupting scene that fused hip-hop and skateboarding under the guidance of a style-conscious youth.

The brand's OG gorilla logo is a homage to style in its own right, borrowing the curved lines and gorilla icon from the original Ben Davis logo, twisting the image and stamping it with the X-Large name. Ben Davis alongside Carhartt WIP was one of the most important influences on what would eventually become a style synonymous with X-Large itself – in which workwear was taken away from its originally intended use and combined with sneakers and other accessories to create a look that was for the streets, not for construction sites. The Beastie Boys' Mike D was an influential part of the brand's foundations and the group would be a huge vehicle for perpetuating X-Large's appeal throughout the 1990s, with Mike D rarely seen without a piece of X-Large clothing in the group's many public appearances and music videos.

This new look sparked the beginning of the streetwear 'scene' that would give birth to most of the designs featured in this book. Nothing is more iconic than the X-Large OG logo T-shirt that features the brand's gorilla logo printed large across the chest. Every true streetwear fan needs at least one of these in their collection.

Opposite: The OG (original) logo pays homage to its Ben Davis predecessor.

42 X-Large's original
'Gorilla' design,
a staple of the
brand since its
origins in 1991.

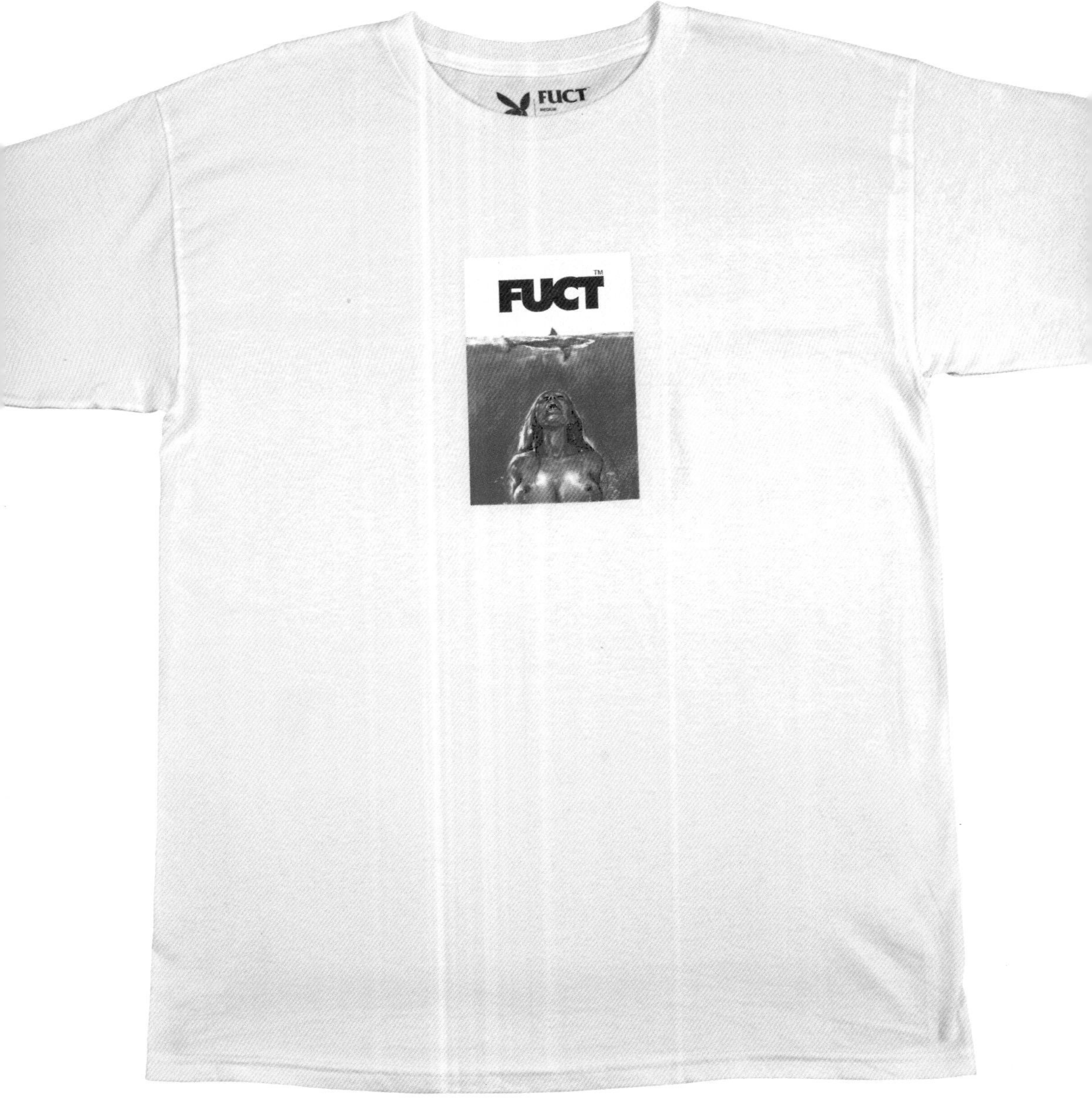
FUCT
FUCT™

Fuct's second contribution to this book features another well-known image flipped on its head, this time using the original artwork from Peter Benchley's *Jaws* novel and Steven Spielberg's 1975 film of the same name. The original art features the story's shark protagonist creeping from below the water, stalking his prey, but Fuct made a few changes to the design to create something truly special.

In Fuct's interpretation, the hunter becomes the hunted as the lone swimmer takes the shark's place under the water (with added nudity for increased shock value) and the shark takes her position on top. The large, red, block text of the *Jaws* logo is, of course, changed to read Fuct, too, but the style of the original poster is kept intact.

There's some unconfirmed subtext here about the dangers of a strong-willed woman who's not just a maneater but fierce enough to take down a Great White, but we prefer to appreciate this particular piece for its parodic approach to pop culture. The 'Jawz' T-shirt was a huge success for Fuct and has returned to the line several times since its original release in 1992. It's a great example of pop-cultural appropriation in streetwear, something that was pioneered by Fuct founder Erik Brunetti and which would become a vital element in many iconic streetwear T-shirts in the years to follow.

Fuct
'Jawz'

1992

The Shorty's brand and imagery are full of nostalgia for anyone who was interested in skateboarding in the 1990s. In 1992 Shorty's was born out of an idea to create shorter skateboard bolts for those who no longer wished to use risers, and soon enough a new industry standard had been created.

Shorty's developed its product range to include griptape, bearings, boards and most other skateboard hardware. Like many skateboard brands, Shorty's also produced branded apparel as promotional materials to be worn by its team of riders and help bring additional attention to the brand. Shorty's owed a lot of its popularity to pro skateboarder Chad Muska, a rising star who was known for his outlandish fashion sense. In 1998 Muska appeared in Shorty's 'Fulfill the Dream' video (remembered for the section where he can be seen skating with one arm around a boombox), and could be seen wearing the classic Shorty's logo T-shirt several times throughout.

The Shorty's logo design was based on the branding of its hand-made bolt display boxes – a rectangular box with Shorty's text running diagonally across the centre. The brand's association with Chad Muska helped Shorty's sell a lot of skateboards, but also a great deal of T-shirts, and this particular design is remembered as one of the great images of nineties skateboarding.

Opposite: 47
Shorty's logo design was based on the branding of its hand-made bolt display boxes.

Shorty's logo

1992

Girl Skateboards logo

1993

Girl Skateboards was established in 1993 by friends and pro skateboarders Mike Carroll and Rick Howard after they both chose to leave their then sponsors to set up on their own. Both Carroll and Howard had become disenchanted by the goings-on in the industry at the time and set out to create a company that operated under their own rules.

The Girl logo, recognizable as the symbol used worldwide to identify a women's bathroom, was created by Girl in-house artist Andy Jenkins. Jenkins heads up Girl's now-legendary 'Art Dump' art department, which has been a major influence on skateboard art in the years since Girl's inception, thanks to a long list of decorated contributors that includes Kevin Lyons, Andy Mueller and Spike Jonze.

Original Girl Skateboards logo T-shirts featured a small, centralized chest graphic – a true marker of nineties T-shirt design that has more recently been replaced with much larger screen-printed graphics. T-shirts were available in a variety of colours and featured the Girl logo surrounded by a rectangular box, as it would on any toilet door. Skateboarding is notoriously a male-dominated industry, and so the decision to use this symbol as the central logo for its brand gave Girl something unique, and reminded wearers that they should never take life too seriously.

Opposite: With skateboarding such a notoriously male-dominated industry, the decision to use this logo gave Girl something unique.

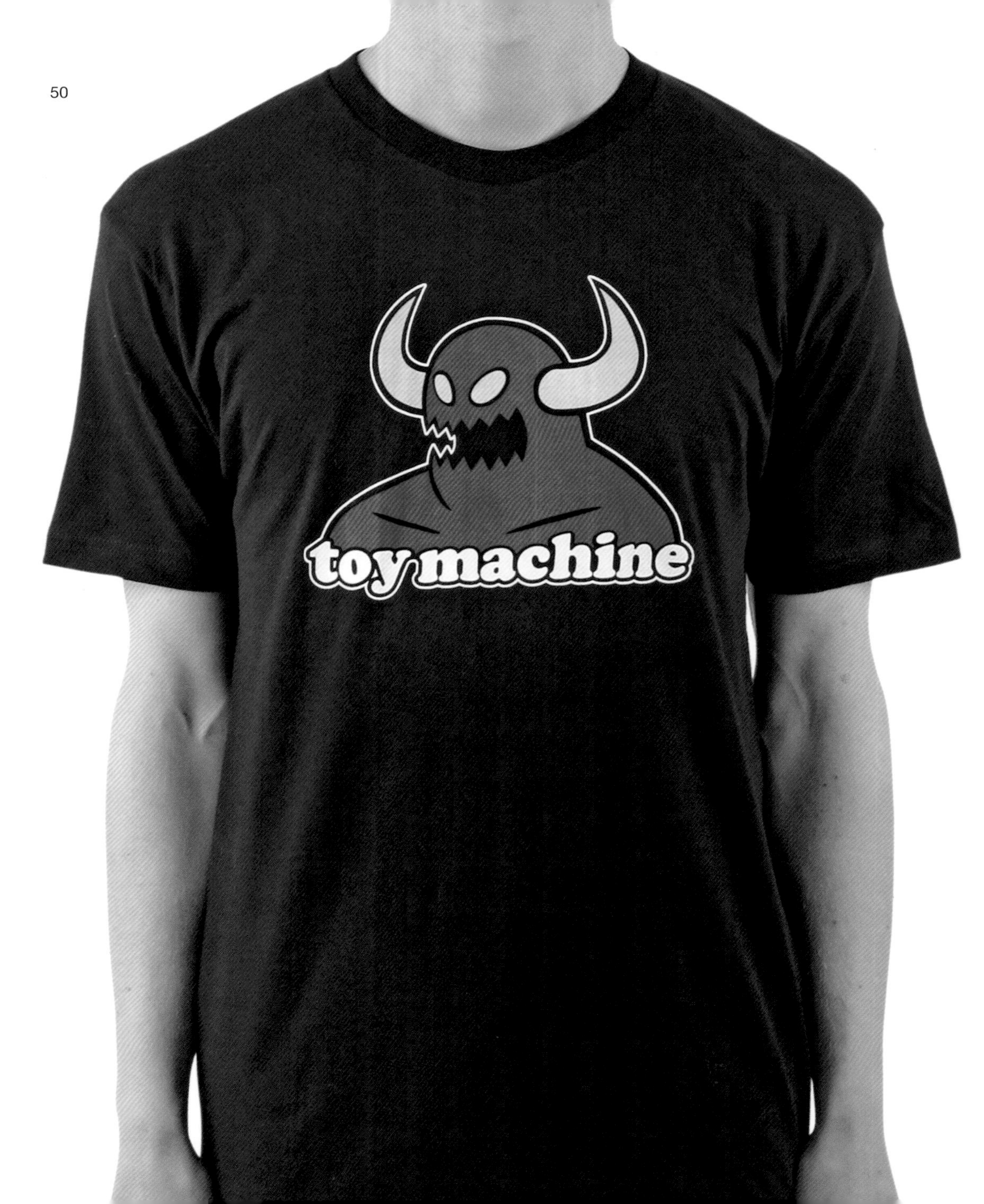
toy machine

Ed Templeton's Toy Machine Monster logo is a familiar image for anyone who experienced skateboarding in the 1990s. The company was established by Templeton in 1993 through a relationship with Vision Street Wear's Brad Dorfman and eventually with support from Tum Yeto distribution owner Tod Swank. All of the company's artwork was created by Templeton.

Templeton had been inspired by skate artists like Mark Gonzales who created their own board graphics. Central to the brand was the Monster, a red, devil-like creature with jagged teeth and bright-yellow eyes. As well as appearing on skateboard decks, the Monster graphic made its way on to T-shirts and other Toy Machine apparel and became a common sight throughout the 1990s. Like other designs of the time, the Toy Machine graphics were smaller than most today and centred across the chest, carrying with them a distinct nineties flavour.

The Toy Machine Monster is almost always portrayed in its signature red-and-yellow colour scheme, with few exceptions. Like Spitfire and other brands that have adopted cartoon mascots, the bold and colourful designs have helped Toy Machine appeal to a younger audience. His work with Toy Machine has led to Ed Templeton becoming one of the most respected artists in skateboarding today and the brand continues to release new products regularly.

Opposite: The Monster, a devil-like creature with jagged teeth and bright-yellow eyes, was designed by Toy Machine founder Ed Templeton.

51

Toy Machine Monster logo

1993

In 1993 A Bathing Ape, now better known as BAPE, put into place a number of practices that are commonplace in streetwear today and integral elements of any successful brand. While brands like Stüssy, Fuct and X-Large were heading up the Western streetwear movement, BAPE was created in Japan and brought with it its own unique flavour.

The brand was the idea of Tomoaki Nagao, known as 'Nigo', who began printing limited runs of T-shirts to sell at his Nowhere store in the Harajuku area of Shibuya, Tokyo. These quickly became very popular. Limited-issue products would become a very important part of the BAPE brand, which chose to avoid traditional advertising and wholesale routes and sold its products only through its own BAPE stores in small numbers. The Ape Head logo, a simplified drawing of a gorilla's head, would become central to the brand, and collectors would seek it out on T-shirts, jackets, accessories and all manner of BAPE products.

One particularly popular version of the Ape Head logo is printed in full colour on a white T-shirt with no other branding, just the registered trademark symbol. Thanks to their premium quality and limited availability, BAPE designs were a popular choice for a number of hip-hop artists, notably Kanye West and Pharrell Williams, the latter of whom went on to work with Nigo to produce the Billionaire Boys Club (see pages 84–5) and Ice Cream brands.

Opposite: The Ape Head logo is central to the BAPE brand and collectors continue to seek it out on all manner of products.

BAPE
Ape Head logo

1993

Alife
'Ain't Alife Grand'

1999

Alife's range of staple logo T-shirts is a great piece of streetwear history. It's rare that a brand is held in such high regard that fans will be desperate to seek out a simple text logo design with almost no embellishment carrying the brand name, but the 'Ain't Alife Grand' T-shirt from New York's Alife was just that.

The Alife story began in New York in 1999 out of a small retail space on Orchard Street. The store quickly became an important destination for limited-edition sneakers and premium apparel, and the team's work as a creative agency behind the scenes brought Alife international recognition among the industry's biggest players. Alife is now known for its full clothing collection, rooted in graphic T-shirts and sweatshirts, as well as a number of high-profile footwear collaborations with the likes of New Balance, Puma and Reebok.

The Alife text logo became a symbol for those in the know when it came to sneakers and exclusive streetwear. The brand's name was transformed in various ways, but almost always displayed as simple lettering across the chest of T-shirts in a multitude of colours. One great example is the 'Ain't Alife Grand design', which plays on the brand's name in large, statement-making letters across the chest of a classic white T-shirt. These T-shirt designs still represent the backbone of the brand and are available from its stores in New York and Japan as well as other respected streetwear and sneaker stores all over the world.

Opposite: The 'Ain't Alife Grand' design is a great example of the huge range of logo-based T-shirts that form the backbone of the brand.

The OBEY name is now most often associated with the clothing line formed in 2000, but its story began back in 1989 with the early efforts of artist Shepard Fairey.

While studying at the Rhode Island School of Design, the 19-year-old began printing stickers featuring an image of seven-foot-four professional wrestler André René Roussimoff, better known as 'André the Giant'. The stickers were distributed throughout the school's campus, the surrounding streets and nearby cities, and helped Fairey achieve a level of infamy as a young artist. Fairey continued to pursue his art, moving from stickers to larger artworks including the OBEY 'Giant' design featured on the 'Icon Face' T-shirt.

Founded in 2000, the OBEY Clothing label gave Shepard Fairey a new canvas on which to display his work. The rectangular design on the 'Icon Face' T-shirt features the image of André the Giant from Fairey's original sticker campaign, but reworked so that it became almost unrecognizable. Below it sits OBEY's block Red Bar logo, an equally popular design for the brand when printed on its own. Both the black-and-white palette and the Red Bar logo are inspired by the work of American conceptual artist Barbara Kruger and the bold statements that adorn her work. Kruger's work is of particular importance to streetwear, inspiring designs of many other brands like Supreme and Alife, and Shepard Fairey openly cites the artist as one of his biggest influences.

Opposite: The rectangular design on the 'Icon Face' T-shirt is based on an image of professional wrestler André the Giant by artist Shepard Fairey.

OBEY
'Icon Face'

2000

Fucking Awesome logo

The story of Fucking Awesome began with two friends, Jason Dill and Mike Piscitelli, in a New York apartment in 2001. Like many other brands of its kind, Fucking Awesome was started almost unintentionally, as a do-it-yourself avenue for an overabundance of creative energy, caused at least in part by a penchant for illegal substances. The pair began printing T-shirts to distribute among friends, although the involvement of pro skateboarder Dill soon elevated the brand to a higher level of demand.

Piscitelli's move back to California gave the brand a foothold on each coast and the Fucking Awesome word continued to spread. Fucking Awesome was anti-streetwear in many ways, with the pair never looking to fit the traditional mould. Both Dill and Piscitelli had other jobs, which meant they were not reliant on the success of the brand, allowing them to take things in a less commercial direction. The designs were bold and controversial, a spirit embodied by the brand's name and plain to see in the Fucking Awesome logo T-shirts – Dill and Piscitelli were not afraid to offend.

The desirability of Fucking Awesome's T-shirts was helped by the fact they were not easy to come by and could be found only at select stores globally. Even today, only a very small number of boutiques carry the Fucking Awesome brand, and its T-shirts remain highly sought after.

Opposite:
Fucking Awesome is known for its bold and controversial designs, a spirit embodied in the brand's name.

Johnny Cupcakes is an icon for the do-it-yourself T-shirt brand owners of the modern streetwear landscape. The story began in 2001 when brand owner Johnny Earle printed his first batch of T-shirts decorated with the nickname given to him by a group of co-workers. The bold cartoon imagery of his earliest designs soon captured the attention of those he came into contact with – both at work and while touring with his band, On Broken Wings – and the brand quickly grew. Johnny Cupcakes's signature design mocked the 'tough-guy' image, replacing the skull with an image of a cupcake atop the crossed bones, creating something that was fun, cute and bizarre in equal parts.

Johnny's first outlet was the trunk of his car, but he has since extended the cupcake theme to a line of pretend bakeries that sell his T-shirts, with locations across the United States and one in the United Kingdom. Johnny Cupcakes T-shirts are stored in refrigerators and curved glass cabinets and often come inside custom packaging designed like cake mix boxes and tins of frosting. The 'Crossbones' graphic remains central to the brand and regularly appears in different forms. Past versions have seen the logo styled as slices of pizza, as slabs of meat and even as the game Operation, with tweezers reaching in to grab the icon from the wearer's chest.

Opposite: The 'Crossbones' graphic, a play on the skull and crossbones, is central to the Johnny Cupcakes brand.

Johnny Cupcakes 'Crossbones'

aNYthing, otherwise known as 'A New York Thing', is a New York-based clothing brand founded by original Supreme employee Aaron Bondaroff. As the name suggests, aNYthing was all about life in New York and the brand has paid homage to the city with many of its designs.

The best example is the brand's 'Original NY Logo' T-shirt, which features aNYthing text screen-printed across the chest. The 'N' and 'Y' in the design are picked out in a different font from the rest of the lettering, referencing the logo of football team the New York Giants. The blue and red colours of the original release also referenced the Giants, but the design has appeared in various other colours since (including blue and orange variations that are a nod to some of New York's other sports teams), and other versions featuring the logos of the Mets and the Yankees.

The aNYthing brand took New York iconography out of the city to stores all over the world, but can also be found at the brand's own New York flagship store in the city's Lower East Side.

Opposite: aNYthing's 'Original NY Logo' T-shirt references the logo and team colours of football team the New York Giants.

aNYthing
'Original NY Logo'

The Undefeated name originated in Los Angeles in 2002, from the minds of founders James Bond and Eddie Cruz. After each being integral parts of other retail businesses, Bond and Cruz came together to open their own sneaker boutique on La Brea, offering an edited selection of footwear from the world's major brands that provided an alternative to the larger chain stores.

Undefeated has since grown beyond a series of stores in just the United States and Japan into a fully fledged clothing brand that sells internationally and is one of the most recognized labels in streetwear. As the name suggests, Undefeated has sports inspirations at its core, with a range that includes varsity jackets and baseball caps alongside a substantial graphic T-shirt offering. More recently, Undefeated has launched its own range of technical sportswear, combining the visual appeal of its lifestyle collection with high-performance materials and technology.

One design that appears time and time again throughout each of its collections is the brand's 5 Strike logo – Undefeated's take on the classic method of keeping score. The logo appears on T-shirts regularly and is often filled with different colours and designs to match each seasonal collection. The 5 Strike logo is Undefeated's main branding and can be found across all of its stores, its products and also its footwear models produced in collaboration with the world's biggest sports brands.

Opposite: Undefeated's 5 Strike logo is its take on the classic method of keeping score – a reference to the brand's athletic inspirations.

Undefeated
5 Strike logo

2002

HUF
'Skyline'

2002

Formerly San Francisco, now Los Angeles-based skate brand HUF has often paid homage to its Californian roots with its T-shirt designs. The most iconic of these is the 'Skyline' design, alternatively referred to as the 'Etch A Sketch' T-shirt for the single-line drawing style similar to that used by the children's mechanical toy. Two versions of the design exist: one simply displays the HUF logo while the second is an impressive drawing of the San Francisco skyline. Both are made from one single, continuous line.

The designs were reissued in 2012 as part of a collaboration with Benny Gold, the brand run by the former HUF designer who was responsible for designing the Etch A Sketch logo ten years prior. Benny Gold is known in the industry as an exceptionally talented artist and this piece in particular is an excellent example of his graphic design prowess. Said to represent the clean lines and minimal construction of HUF's original San Francisco store, it couldn't be simpler, but it remains one of HUF's most popular products to this day.

Named after its founder, pro skateboarder Keith Hufnagel, HUF began life as a retail store in the Tenderloin District of San Francisco, stocking hard-to-find products from the world's premier skate, streetwear and sneaker brands. It would soon evolve into a custom clothing line known for its T-shirts, hats, accessories and, more recently, footwear, and for hosting its own skate team made up of some of the world's biggest pros.

Opposite and below: HUF paid homage to its Californian roots with its 'Etch A Sketch' style 'Skyline' design and logo T-shirts.

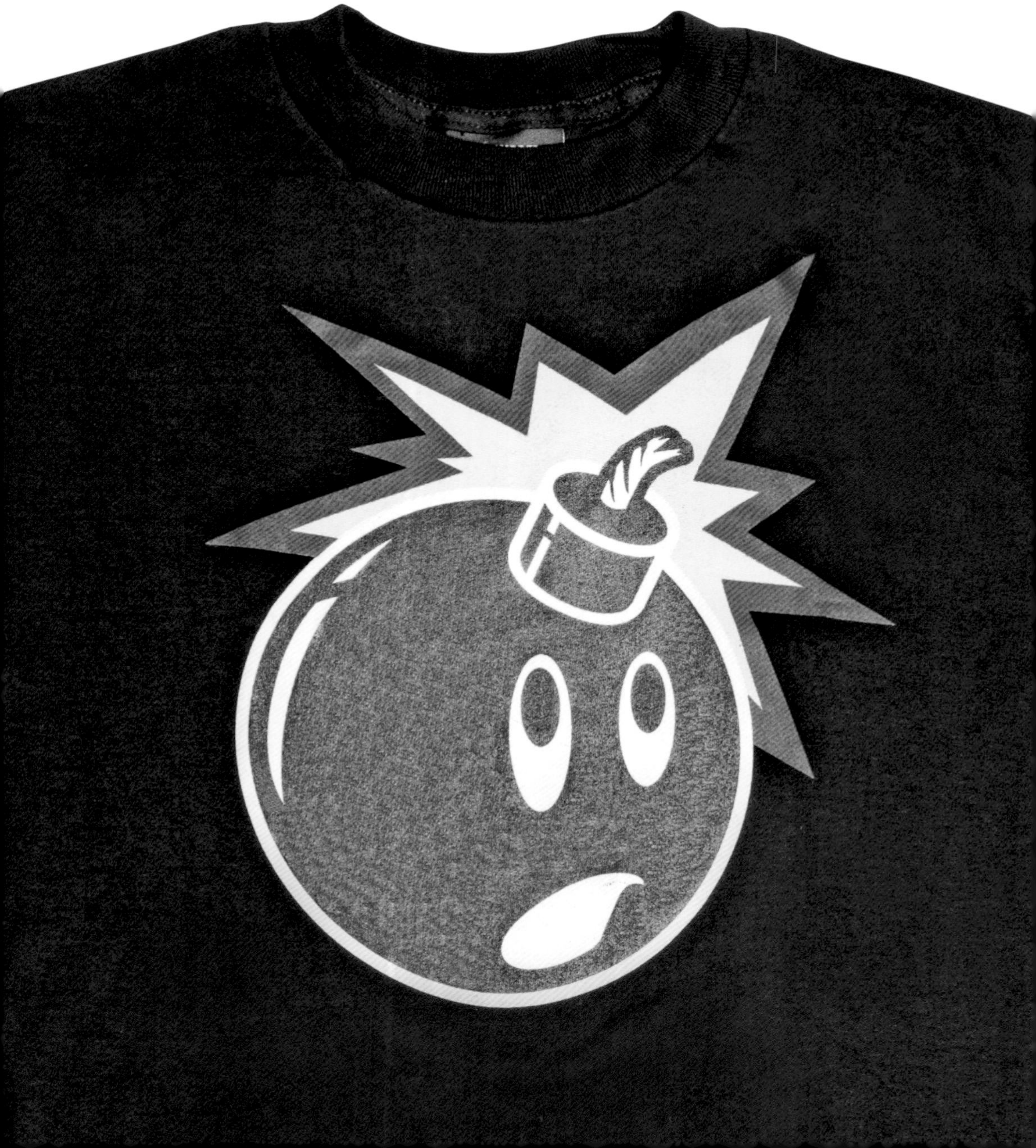

The Adam Bomb character has for a long time been the mascot of the The Hundreds brand. The round cartoon bomb, complete with exploding fuse, is central to many of the brand's bold and colourful designs that have helped The Hundreds appeal to a huge global audience. Appearing in various colours, forms and designs throughout the brand's history, many collectors will have a few variations in their collections. What many do not have though is the 'Black Adam' design – a plain black T-shirt featuring the full-colour, unmodified Adam Bomb design.

For many years these 'Black Adam' T-shirts existed purely as gifts to certified members of The Hundreds' family, with only a handful in existence. The money-can't-buy design became one of the brand's most sought after, but remained unattainable for even the most hardcore collectors for many years. On the opening of the brand's Santa Monica flagship store in 2011 the first 50 customers in line were each given a 'Black Adam' T-shirt as a thank-you for their loyalty and support. Since then the mythical 'Black Adam' T-shirt has disappeared back into the brand's archives and we may never see it again.

Founded by friends Ben and Bobby in 2003, The Hundreds represents Los Angeles lifestyle to the fullest, with many of the brand's designs referencing classic elements of Californian culture. With flagship stores in Los Angeles, Santa Monica, San Francisco and New York, The Hundreds is known for its creative T-shirt designs, headwear and accessories.

Opposite: The Hundreds' mythical 'Black Adam' T-shirt is one of the brand's hardest-to-find and most sought-after designs.

71

The Hundreds 'Black Adam'

2003

Mishka
Keep Watch logo

Mishka's Keep Watch graphic is without a doubt one of the most iconic of its breed in streetwear. Strong and simple, the Keep Watch design forgoes the more conventional option of using the brand name, in exchange for a large cartoon eyeball that has appeared in an endless list of colours and forms since the brand's inception in 2003.

The Keep Watch graphic forms part of a series of characters in Mishka's logo-arsenal and brings together some of the horror-film and comic-book influences that run through the brand's core. The most classic of these iterations – found on the shelves of skate and streetwear stores the world over – is a bloodshot eye with a sky-blue iris staring menacingly from the centre of a white T-shirt.

Mishka's close ties to electronic dance music and prominent DJs across the world have lead to the design becoming a fantastic travelling billboard for the brand. Combined with a baseball cap featuring the same eyeball design on the front of the crown and a gaping mouth complete with fanged teeth under the peak, the Keep Watch logo would become Mishka's signature and would help the brand to be recognized all over the world.

Mishka was founded by partners Greg Rivera and Mikhail Bortnik in Brooklyn, New York in 2003. The brand is distributed internationally and boasts four flagship stores in San Francisco, Los Angeles, Brooklyn and Tokyo.

Opposite: This graphic is part of a series of characters in Mishka's logo-arsenal and has appeared in multiple colours and forms.

The classic
version of the
Keep Watch
logo T-shirt from
Mishka, in white
with red and blue
detailing on the
iconic eyeball.

REBEL8
8 logo

Many of REBEL8's designs are strengthened by the incredible talents of artist Mike Giant, known for his work in graffiti and tattooing as well as a legacy in pen on paper. Giant founded REBEL8 with partner Joshy D in 2003 as a means of showcasing his gifts in a different medium – one that would eventually take his designs all over the world.

Many of REBEL8's designs are completely hand-drawn rather than generated by computers, which gives them a unique edge – something that is often imitated but never equalled. With REBEL8, Mike Giant gave birth to new ways of bringing tattoo-inspired designs to clothing with his illustrations of barely-clothed girls covered head-to-toe in hand drawn tattoos and by illustrating on top of photoreal prints of models – their clean skin providing the perfect blank canvases.

Where the REBEL8 brand is concerned, nothing is more iconic than its 8 logo, which features a hand-drawn version of the '8' portion of the brand's name complete with a tattoo-style diamond in the centre. The 8 logo has become a symbol for those who identify with the brand's ideology, with many fans choosing to take the extra step of having the logo tattooed on their body, permanently marking them as members of the REBEL8 family.

Opposite:
The REBEL8 8 logo has become an international symbol for those who identify with the brand's ideology.

The Hundreds
'Hip-Hop is Dead'

2004

The 'Hip-Hop is Dead' design perfectly sums up the spirit of The Hundreds and the brand's passion for making a statement, challenging perceptions and generally sparking a reaction. Many of the designs have a political or social undercurrent, but there is almost always a story behind each individual graphic.

Released in 2004, not long after the brand's initial origins in 2003, the bold statement was the first design to garner the brand significant recognition and helped to elevate The Hundreds to a new level in streetwear. Flipping the age-old 'Punk is Dead' phrase for the early-2000s generation and the brand's own audience, the design became one of The Hundreds' most popular releases and is still one often associated with the brand years later.

The design was printed in white across the chest of a black T-shirt, with the lack of colour amplifying its morbid message and the subtle markings of spray paint and a stencil around the text adding a guerilla feel. Hip-hop was, of course, not dead, but this controversial design finished with images of several dead hip-hop icons on the reverse sparked just the reaction that The Hundreds were hoping for.

In July 2013, marking the end of the brand's tenth anniversary, The Hundreds re-released the 'Hip-Hop is Dead' design as part of a collection of ten favourite designs from the brand's past, selected by its founders, Ben and Bobby.

Opposite: The controversial 'Hip-Hop is Dead' T-shirt was the first design to garner The Hundreds significant recognition.

British brand maharishi is synonymous with camouflage, and the brand's creative director, Hardy Blechman, is known as one of the world's foremost experts on the subject. In 2004 Blechman released the encyclopedic book *DPM: Disruptive Pattern Material* after almost seven years of research into the history of camouflage, starting with its place in nature, through its military uses, to more modern adaptations in fashion. The book came wrapped in a camouflage cover with a fluorescent-orange band surrounding it front to back. Now out of print, *DPM* is very hard to come by, though much sought after by collectors. The camouflage used was a woodland example used by the British Armed Forces.

Maharishi regularly utilizes camouflage in its designs, and several camo T-shirts have been released throughout the brand's history. This particular piece mimics the design of the *DPM* book, with the same woodland camouflage used all over and the orange wrap covering both sides. The 'DPM' text is placed on the chest with additional details on the back of the T-shirt that also match the book's design.

Camo is a hugely important element of streetwear design, and many modern brands owe a lot to the work of Blechman and the designs released by maharishi. This T-shirt marks an important moment in streetwear history that will go on to influence many brands in the future.

maharishi
'British DPM'

2004

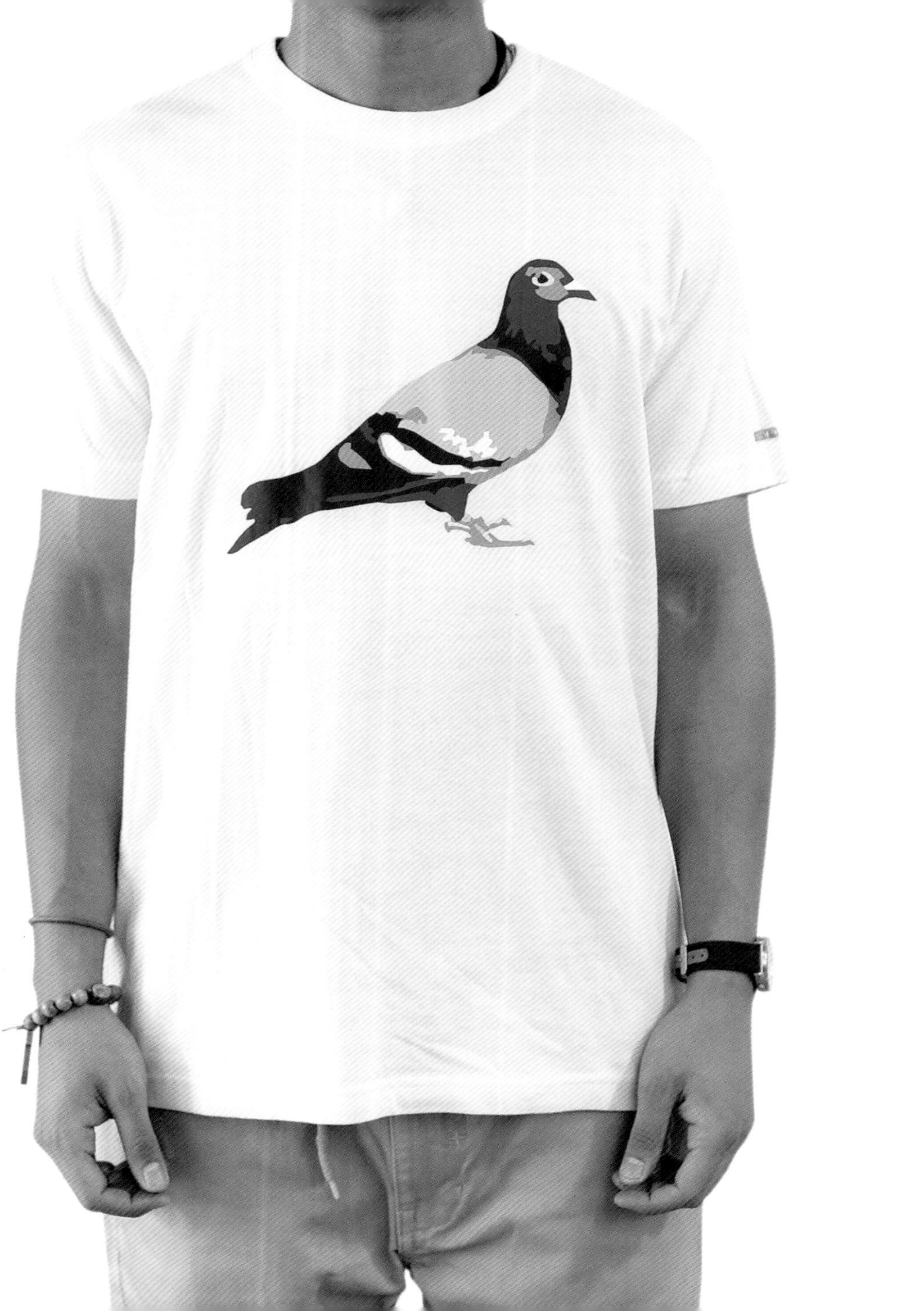

Staple's Pigeon icon is one of the most infamous in streetwear and sneaker history and a nod to the New York streets where the brand, founded by graphic designer Jeff Ng, was born. Jeff put together the first Staple T-shirts in 1997, which were sold in various boutiques around New York City before Staple opened its own retail store, Reed Space, in 2002.

The Pigeon icon became the stuff of legend following Staple's collaboration project with Nike SB in 2005 on the Dunk Low Pro 'Pigeon'. The shoe's colourway took inspiration from the recognizable colours of the pigeon – two shades of grey mimicking the bird's feathers with a pink outsole tread matching the feet. The image of a pigeon was embroidered on to the heel of each shoe and would become an important icon for sneaker collectors and streetwear fans in the years to come. A small number of pairs were released at the Reed Space store, where there was huge anticipation, drawing crowds that massively outweighed the supply. Riots erupted in the streets, the police were called in and several weapons were found, wielded by those hoping to strip those fortunate enough to have got hold of a pair.

The story made front-page news in the days following and remains one of the legendary moments in sneaker history. The 'Pigeon' T-shirt was released the same day, featuring a screen-printed image of the Pigeon logo in matching colours of white, grey and pink, and was a little easier to get hold of. Since 2005, Staple has released a series of pigeon-themed products and sneakers, including other footwear collaborations with New Balance, PUMA and Converse.

Staple 'Pigeon'

2005

The Billionaire Boys Club brand, often called BBC for short, was established in 2005 by Pharrell Williams as he embarked on a career as a solo artist away from his work as part of The Neptunes and N.E.R.D. Partnering with friend and BAPE creator Nigo, Pharrell created a line of premium products with a fairly high price tag – reflected in the company's name, a club only for the wealthy.

The BBC range centred around a number of recurring logos and characters, including this classic Arch logo. Since its origins in 2005 the Arch logo has appeared in almost every colour imaginable on the chests of T-shirts and sweatshirts. The design features the brand name in arched form, accompanied by the helmeted head of the BBC Astronaut – another recurring character in the brand's line.

Wearing one of these designs identified the wearer as a member of an exclusive club. Pharrell could regularly be spotted in an Arch logo T-shirt himself, as could his legion of famous friends including Jay-Z, Lil Wayne and Drake. The celebrity association has helped maintain the popularity of the design over the years and it remains one of the brand's most popular products.

Opposite: The Billionaire Boys Club range centres around a number of recurring logos and characters, including this classic Arch logo.

Billionaire Boys Club Arch logo

2005

A handful of variations of the Billionaire Boys Club Arch logo that have been issued throughout the brand's history.

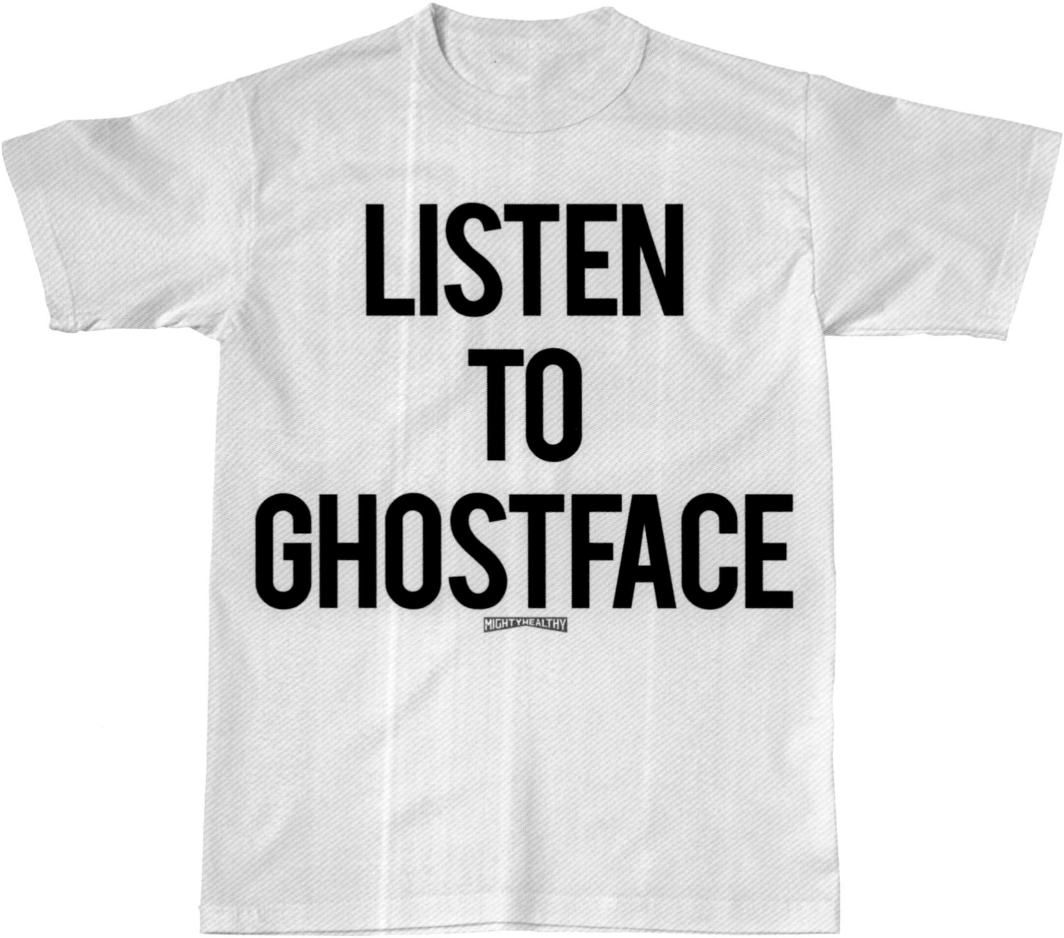
LISTEN
TO
GHOSTFACE
MIGHTYHEALTHY

New York brand Mighty Healthy was founded in 2004 by avid streetwear fan and skateboarder Ray Mate, who brought together his love of skateboarding with his own interest in apparel to create a new T-shirt brand rooted in New York street culture. Over the years Mighty Healthy has released an extensive collection of graphic T-shirts and have become especially well known for its 'Listen To …' series of designs.

The T-shirts each feature 'Listen To …' text printed large across the chest, followed by the name of a different band or artist of significance and, of course, the Mighty Healthy logo. Popular versions of the design include Biggie, U.G.K. and Slayer, showcasing a diverse range of musical influences, but with a particular focus on hip-hop.

The variation that the brand is best known for, however, is the 'Listen To Ghostface' T-shirt, which brought Mighty Healthy a lot of attention when first released in 2006. The brand itself is named after a song by Ghostface Killah, released on his 2000 album *Supreme Clientele*. It was only right that Mighty Healthy pay homage to the artist with a T-shirt of his own and it is fitting that it has become one of the brand's most popular.

Opposite: Naming the T-shirt after a Ghostface Killah song, Mighty Healthy here paid homage to the Wu-Tang Clan member.

Mighty Healthy
'Listen To Ghostface'

2006

The 'Gun Show' design by Los Angeles brand Rogue Status is certainly iconic for its period in the mid-2000s and like The Hundreds' 'Paisley' T-shirt (see pages 92–3) it is a great reminder of a time when all-over prints ruled streetwear design. The 'Gun Show' concept was simple – a detailed pattern of handguns, shotguns, rocket launchers and all manner of automatic weapons, lined up and repeated across the entirety of the T-shirt body. The juxtaposition of a relatively minimal design with such shocking imagery is what makes this T-shirt stand out from the rest of the Rogue Status collection and allowed the 'Gun Show' print to make a significant mark on streetwear history.

The all-over print was all about grabbing attention and with this design Rogue Status took that one step further. The 'Gun Show' print is also remembered for the vast extent of its offering, available on T-shirts, hoodies and jackets in almost every colour combination imaginable. The bright and playful colours often used on 'Gun Show' T-shirts further added to the contrast of the design – it was quite bizarre to see such violent and destructive weapons printed in pink and purple, but this has only added to the lasting impression that the 'Gun Show' design has made.

Rogue Status utilized the design for a number of years before moving on, rebranding as DTA Posse, and the infamous 'Gun Show' print is now no more.

Opposite: The 'Gun Show' design by Los Angeles brand Rogue Status is a great reminder of a time when all-over prints ruled streetwear design.

Rogue Status 'Gun Show'

2006

The all-over print holds its place in time, documenting a period in mid-2000s streetwear that was all about being loud. Moving away from the smaller graphic styles of the 1990s, popularized by brands like Fuct and Supreme, a new breed of streetwear brands formed in the early 2000s that made their presence known with bold, statement-making designs.

The 'Paisley' design from The Hundreds is among the most revered, releasing first as a print across the outside of a zip-hoodie before making its way on to T-shirts. It featured a repeating paisley pattern across front and back and was available in a variety of colours before selling out very quickly. The designs were traded heavily on online forums as collectors hunted out colours they might have missed or tried to make a quick buck from those who had been slow to catch on.

The all-over print trend has come and gone, but this particular design would still make a splash were it ever to return for sale. The Hundreds revisited the all-over print theme with its 2011 collaboration with Diamond Supply Co., which included a number of designs featuring a Hawaiian-holiday-style print. Releasing in November, the range was a striking contrast to the styles normally expected during the winter months and a great nod to the brand's long-time followers who would remember some of its earliest efforts.

The Hundreds 'Paisley'

2006

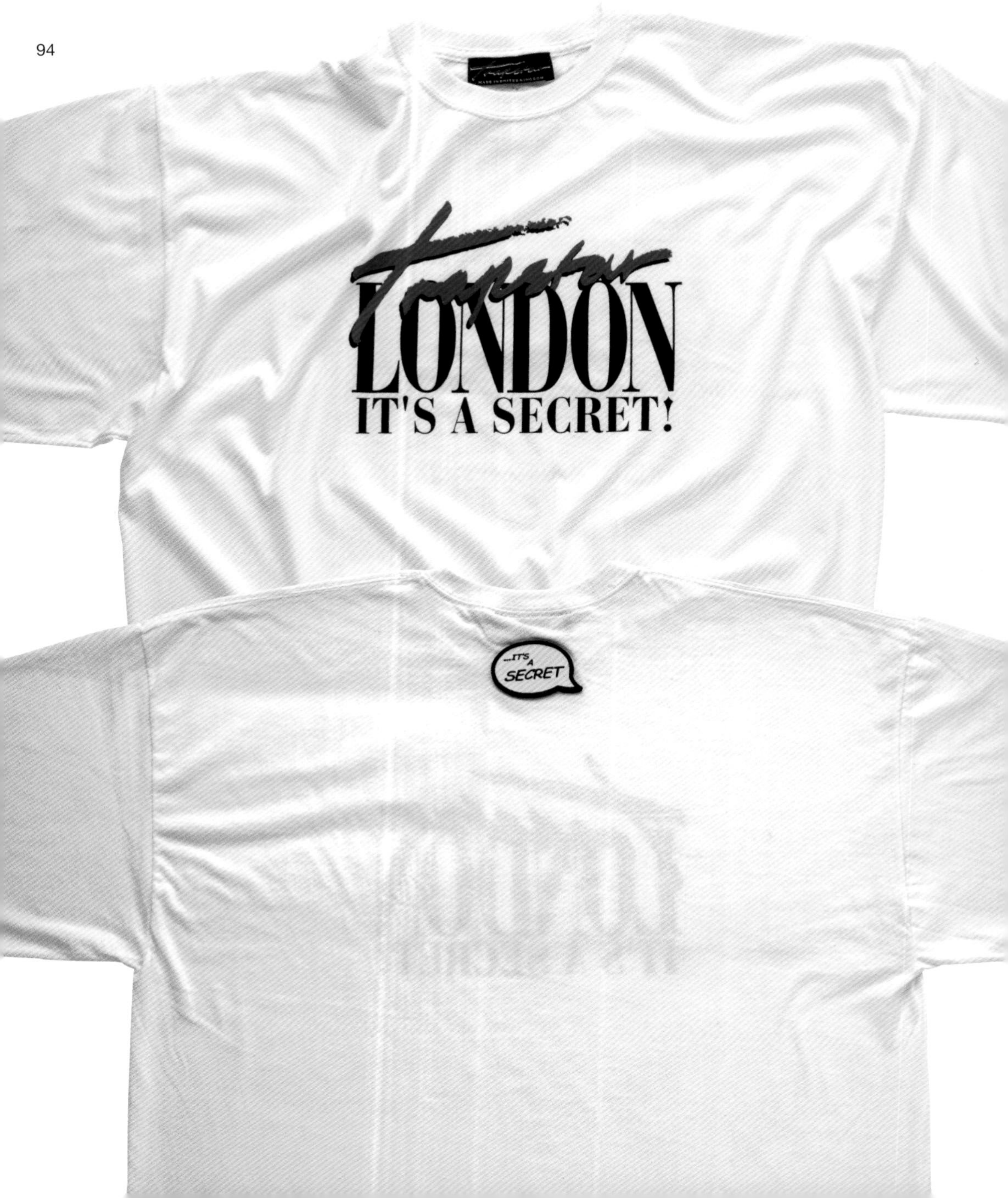
LONDON
IT'S A SECRET!
...IT'S A SECRET

Trapstar is leading the way for modern British streetwear. Developed on the streets of London, Trapstar took inspiration from the larger US brands to create something that London youth could get behind. Now a favourite of everyone from Jay-Z to Rihanna, Trapstar is on the global stage, flying the flag for the UK.

What made Trapstar's early efforts special was the delivery method. The 'It's A Secret' tagline ran on most of the brand's products, signifying that those who knew of the brand's existence were part of an exclusive club. Trapstar products were rarely available for sale in stores or online and were instead sold at a handful of 'Invasion' events, popping up in various locations for one day only. These events had to be sought out and those who missed them might have to wait months before another opportunity came their way.

The 'It's A Secret' design featured a number of elements that were key to the brand – the red Trapstar script, the London stamp and, of course, the 'It's A Secret' tag. Produced in the brand's signature black, white and red colour combination, it would become one of its most popular designs and featured regularly on T-shirts, sweatshirts and hoodies. Early versions were finished with a Velcro 'It's A Secret' speech bubble patch between the shoulders on the back, and this, together with the branded 'pizza box' packaging, added to the new owner's belief that they were getting something special with every purchase.

Opposite: The 'It's A Secret' design features elements that are key to the brand – the red Trapstar script, the London stamp and the 'It's A Secret' tagline.

95

Trapstar
'It's A Secret'

2006

Crooks & Castles
Medusa logo

2007

We've already seen a few examples of streetwear designers appropriating the logos of better-known brands and making them their own, but Crooks & Castles – part of streetwear's new age alongside brands like The Hundreds and Diamond Supply Co. – brought new definition to this trend with the introduction of its Medusa logo.

Taking the iconic and instantly recognizable branding of Versace, Crooks gave Medusa a significant twist by throwing a bandana across her face – a complete flip on the luxury feel carried by the original, creating something new for the streets. The design was an instant hit and brought the brand a lot of attention. It played into the aspirational feel that Crooks were seeking when the brand was first created in Los Angeles in 2002 and helped cement them as a major player in a newly energized streetwear scene on the West Coast.

Inspired by the Los Angeles brands that had come before them, Crooks offered a darker take on streetwear with an additional focus on quality production. The Medusa logo was central to the brand's early years and has appeared in countless variations since. Recent versions of the design have differed significantly from the original Versace inspiration, including those picturing Medusa with the whole head of snakes with which she is more often portrayed.

Opposite:
Taking the iconic branding of Versace, Crooks & Castles gave Medusa a significant twist.

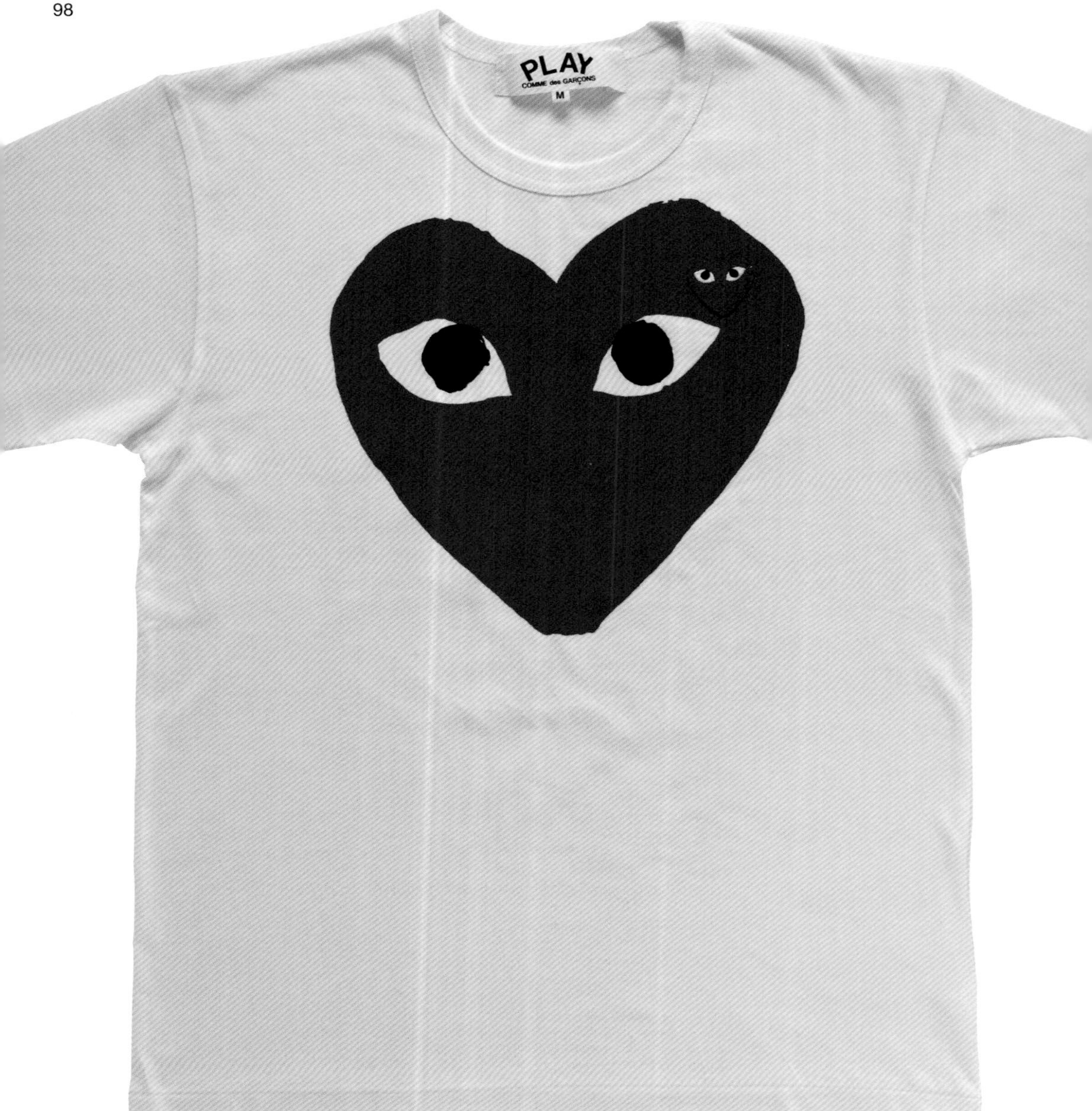
PLAY
COMME des GARÇONS
M

The Play range is a sub-label of Japanese fashion brand Comme des Garçons, established by designer Rei Kawakubo. Play represents the more casual, graphic end of Comme des Garçons, with almost all pieces featuring the signature Heart logo.

The Play logo is a hand-painted red heart with two eyes staring from its centre. It was designed by New York-based Polish artist Filip Pagowski whose initial connection to the brand was through modelling. Although not originally intended for the Play line, the heart would eventually become the mascot of that collection when it launched in 2002. As the story goes, the original design was a completely spontaneous painting and the logo that was chosen and is still in use today is from the first ever draft, with little to no reworking.

The Play label has produced several collaborations, including a 2012 project with A Bathing Ape on several T-shirt designs and an ongoing partnership with Converse that sees the Heart logo regularly feature on Hi and Low versions of the classic 'Chuck Taylor' sneaker. The white logo T-shirt remains the most popular version of the design, though, and has been endorsed publicly by the likes of Pharrell Williams and Kanye West with many other famous faces regularly seen wearing Play designs.

Comme des Garçons Play Heart logo

2007

While most of the T-shirts featured in this book come from US brands and designers, there are a few notable exceptions. One particular highlight from the archives of British streetwear is the 'Weather Pattern' T-shirt from the London-based Second Son.

Mixing the graphic styling of its US contemporaries with unique elements of British culture, Second Son created something special with its T-shirt designs, helping to solidify Great Britain's place in the streetwear story. The brand was started out of London's legendary streetwear stronghold Bond International, where designer Will Kemp had worked surrounded by product from US brands. With Loki (the brand's original name) and eventually Second Son, Kemp and partner Rufus Exton created the perfect response, loaded with a very British sense of humour.

The 'Weather Pattern' design featured a repeating motif of clouds and lightning (the kind seen on TV weather forecasts) printed across the chest of T-shirts in a variety of colours. It poked fun at the traditionally dull and miserable British weather, in stark contrast to the sunny Californian climate that nurtured brands like Stüssy and other US streetwear originators.

The design was first issued under the Loki name in 2005, but when the brand developed into Second Son in 2007 the popularity of 'Weather Pattern' meant that this was one of the designs that were brought along, and has remained available throughout the brand's existence.

Opposite: Second Son's 'Weather Pattern' T-shirt pokes fun at the traditionally dull and miserable British weather.

101

Second Son
'Weather Pattern'

2007

Pigalle
Box logo

2008

The popularity of the logo T-shirt from Parisian store and brand Pigalle owed a lot to streetwear's fascination with high fashion. The Pigalle store offered a small but carefully curated selection of brands and products, hand-picked by founder Stéphane Ashpool who had grown up in the Pigalle area of the city.

The products sold in store were the best of the best, which meant that there was often a premium price tag attached. Pigalle's printed T-shirts presented an affordable option that could easily be purchased by those who wanted to buy into the Pigalle name but didn't have hundreds (or thousands) to spend. The logo featured simple, underlined lettering surrounded by a rectangular box standing out in contrast to the T-shirt body.

The design was a favourite of rapper A$AP Rocky, who would become the unofficial front man of the brand's high-fashion trend, helping to boost its popularity even further. For Pigalle's 2014 collaborative collection with Nike, new T-shirts were produced that replaced the Pigalle name with Nike Air text on T-shirts as well as a range of tank tops, shorts and two premium leather versions of the Nike Air Force 1. The design has appeared in only a handful of other forms, including a limited yellow-and-black version produced for London's Selfridges department store the same year, to match the store's trademark shopping bags.

Opposite: Pigalle's T-shirts presented an affordable option for those who wanted to buy into the Pigalle name but without the premium price tag.

Scratch Free
¡No Raya!

ADDICT ®
with **BLEACH**

Power Cleanser

LIMPIADOR EN POLVO
CON BLANQUEADOR

CAUTION: IRRITANT
NO INSTRUCTIONS OR PRECAUTIONS

PRECAUCION: IRRITANTE
NO HAY INSTRUCCIONES O PRECAUCIONES

NET WT: HEAVY

A Freshjive Formula

When it comes to British streetwear, Chris Carden-Jones's Addict is one of the most recognized names. Founded in Southampton on the UK's south coast in 1994, Addict sought to create a British alternative to the US names that were in command at the time, in particular brands like Fuct, Freshjive and X-Large.

Addict had humble beginnings, printing its designs locally and even hand-dyeing T-shirt bodies to the desired colours. The brand fed a number of truly British elements into its work, taking inspiration from British dance music and Football Casuals subcultures to create something unique. Addict is also known for its partnerships and collaborations with a long list of British artists such as C-Law, sheOne, Swifty and many others.

In 2008 Addict launched the Originator series to pay homage to the brands that had helped forge its original inspiration. Working in collaboration with Fuct, Freshjive and X-Large, Addict produced its own takes on designs from each brand's archive. The highlight of the series was the 'Jive Formula' design, which spun Freshjive's iconic 'Tide' graphic (itself a flip on the Tide laundry detergent logo) into an 'Addict with Bleach' soapbox.

Available in black, white and blue with bold red and yellow print, the design created a great-looking T-shirt that could stand on its own. Those who understood its origins, however, got a little something extra from it.

Opposite: Addict's 'Originator Series' paid homage to the brands that had helped forge its original inspiration, as with its 'Jive Formula' design.

Addict
'Jive Formula'

2008

Palace
Tri-Ferg logo

The arrival of Palace gave British skateboarding a new brand to champion. Billed by many as a UK alternative to revered US brands like Supreme, Palace brought fresh ideas and a do-it-yourself ethos to skateboarding in the UK and it quickly caused a stir. Palace began in 2009 in the scene surrounding London's Slam City Skates, which at the time was one of the only places that the brand's products could be purchased. The original products were produced in strictly limited numbers, meaning that you had to work hard if you wanted a piece for yourself, which only added to the attention that Palace was gaining.

Central to the Palace range is its triangular logo, a version of the Penrose triangle. Put together by British artist Fergus Purcell, better known as Fergadelic, the Tri-Ferg graphic regularly appears on the front and back of T-shirts in various guises, including a limited run of heat-reactive designs like those once issued by Global Hypercolor. The design can also be found on the brand's skateboard hardware products available from select skate stores across the world.

In the years since, Palace has grown to huge popularity outside of skateboarding, thanks in part to some high-profile celebrity endorsements from the likes of Jay-Z and A$AP Rocky and successful collaborations with Reebok and adidas.

Opposite: An example of the Palace Tri-Ferg logo. This version of the Penrose triangle was put together by British artist Fergadelic.

Carhartt WIP's collaboration with luxury Parisian brand A.P.C. presented a premium take on classic workwear styling. Although the brands are quite different, they share commonality in their approach to quality product and attention to detail. The idea for the collaboration was born when the two brands met while opening stores on the same street in Stockholm in 2006, but it wasn't until 2010 that the first in a series of collaborations would become available.

The initial release, centred around a clean pocket T-shirt that bore both Carhartt WIP and A.P.C. branding, sparked a little controversy. The design was a take on the classic Carhartt WIP pocket T-shirt and featured the iconic Carhartt WIP 'C' woven label with the letters 'A' and 'P' printed across the chest and on the pocket, to form the other brand's name. For some it was perfect and summed up both brands' interest in producing quality basics; others deemed it lazy and unconsidered. Regardless, the collaboration was an instant success, with the T-shirt selling out almost immediately in all colour options.

The two brands would go on to work on several collaborative collections in the years following, producing a number of premium versions of workwear staples in luxury materials and, importantly, borrowing A.P.C.'s fit. As a result, the Carhartt WIP + A.P.C. brand has developed a following all of its own.

Opposite: The first collaboration from Carhartt WIP and A.P.C., the design is a take on the classic Carhartt WIP pocket T-shirt plus the letters 'A' and 'P'.

Carhartt WIP + A.P.C. Pocket T-shirt

2010

Stüssy x Stones Throw 'J Dilla'

2010

American hip-hop producer and rapper James 'J Dilla' Yancey sadly passed away in 2006, leaving behind an army of fans and a huge legacy. His influence on hip-hop is unquestionable, and in the years since his death a number of fans have paid tribute to the artist in their own unique ways.

Collaborating with the acclaimed independent record label Stones Throw in 2010, Stüssy paid tribute to the life of J Dilla with two T-shirt designs. The T-shirts both featured a photograph of J Dilla in his converted dining-room studio, originally shot for a book, *Behind the Beat* by Raph Rashid, featuring photographs of the home studios of 28 hip-hop producers.

The photo was shot in 2005, one year prior to J Dilla's death, and shows the artist hard at work while himself wearing a Stüssy T-shirt. Although the photograph is in black and white, on the T-shirt the chain around his neck is highlighted in yellow, which, along with the Stüssy and Stones Throw logos on top, adds an additional element to the original. As a final sign-off, J Dilla's name appears on the back underneath the Stüssy crown, another of the brand's signature icons. The design became one of Stüssy's most popular releases of the 2000s and the limited numbers produced were quick to sell out globally.

Opposite: Stüssy and Stones Throw paid tribute to the life of hip-hop producer and rapper J Dilla with two T-shirt designs.

Nick Tershay's Diamond Supply Co. is well known for a number of reasons. Its 2005 Nike Dunk collaboration remains one of the most collectable to this date, but when it comes to T-shirts Diamond is recognized for a few controversies and legal battles thanks to some highly unapproved parodies, like its 2006 'Runnin' Shit' design that flipped the artwork of Iron Maiden's *The Number of the Beast* album.

Not all of the brand's designs have landed it in trouble, though, and they certainly haven't stopped Diamond becoming one of the biggest-selling streetwear brands across the world. One particular highlight from the brand's back catalogue is its 2010 series featuring singer Cassie Ventura shot by famed portrait photographer Estevan Oriol, printed across the chest of black or white T-shirts. In some of the designs Cassie can be seen to be holding a large diamond with its blue accents picked out in colour against Oriol's greyscale portraits.

The combination of the three well-known names created a huge demand for the release, with designs selling out almost instantly at all retailers. In 2013 Diamond would follow up the release with another design featuring Cassie's portrait in support of her *RockaByeBaby* mixtape.

Opposite: Diamond Supply Co.'s Cassie range features images of singer Cassie Ventura shot by famed portrait photographer Estevan Oriol.

Diamond Supply Co. 'Cassie'

2010

One of the youngest T-shirts in this book comes from the pen and pencil of artist Joe King and Rook, the brand he shares with fellow designer Jonathan Garcia. Having both worked as freelance designers for a number of streetwear greats over many years, the two eventually came together in 2011 to form Rook where they could harness the power of their own talents.

The Notorious B.I.G. (otherwise known as Biggie Smalls) has featured on a huge number of streetwear T-shirts over the years, but Rook's interpretation flipped the script and created something entirely unique. Boosted by the incredible illustrative talents of the brand's lead designer, the 'Biggie Bear' T-shirt took the iconic image of the New York rapper counting cash in a Coogi sweater and replaced Biggie himself with an incredibly detailed illustration of a grizzly bear. As a final touch, Joe took inspiration from a second iconic Biggie image, placing a crooked crown atop the bear's head. While most of the image was left grey to highlight the pencil origins of the design, the jewelled crown and certain parts of the Coogi sweater were highlighted in colour, adding a striking element to the design that allowed it to jump out from the white T-shirt underneath.

A second design known as the 'Peace Big' would follow, showing the Biggie Bear from a second angle, but it was the original that stole the show.

Opposite and following pages: The Notorious B.I.G. has often featured on T-shirts, but Rook's interpretation created something entirely unique.

Rook
'Biggie Bear'

2011

Been Trill is an ambassador for streetwear's modern generation – a market dominated by monochromatic designs, multiple clashing logos and high-fashion inspiration. The brand was formed by a collective of individuals known for being at the forefront of creative thinking and for their command of youth culture. The group includes designers and creative directors Matthew Williams, Virgil Abloh and Heron Preston among others, who are known for their work with artists like Kanye West and Lady Gaga as well as a long list of established global brands.

The Been Trill brand began as a collective name for a group of DJs, but it wasn't long before it evolved into a full clothing collection centred around graphic T-shirts and hats. Many of the brand's designs feature its signature dripping text logo, one that borrows from the title imagery of *The Rocky Horror Picture Show*, with imagery often placed across the front, back and sleeves of T-shirts, covering as much of the printable surface as possible. This multi-print style has become a Been Trill signature and has been regularly imitated since.

One particularly unique element of the Been Trill brand is its ability to sell through both internationally renowned luxury stores like Harvey Nichols and in youth-oriented hubs like American chain PacSun. Only time will tell the legacy that Been Trill will leave behind for a new age of streetwear designers.

Opposite: Many of the Been Trill brand's designs feature its signature dripping text, a logo that borrows from *The Rocky Horror Picture Show*.

Been Trill logo

2012

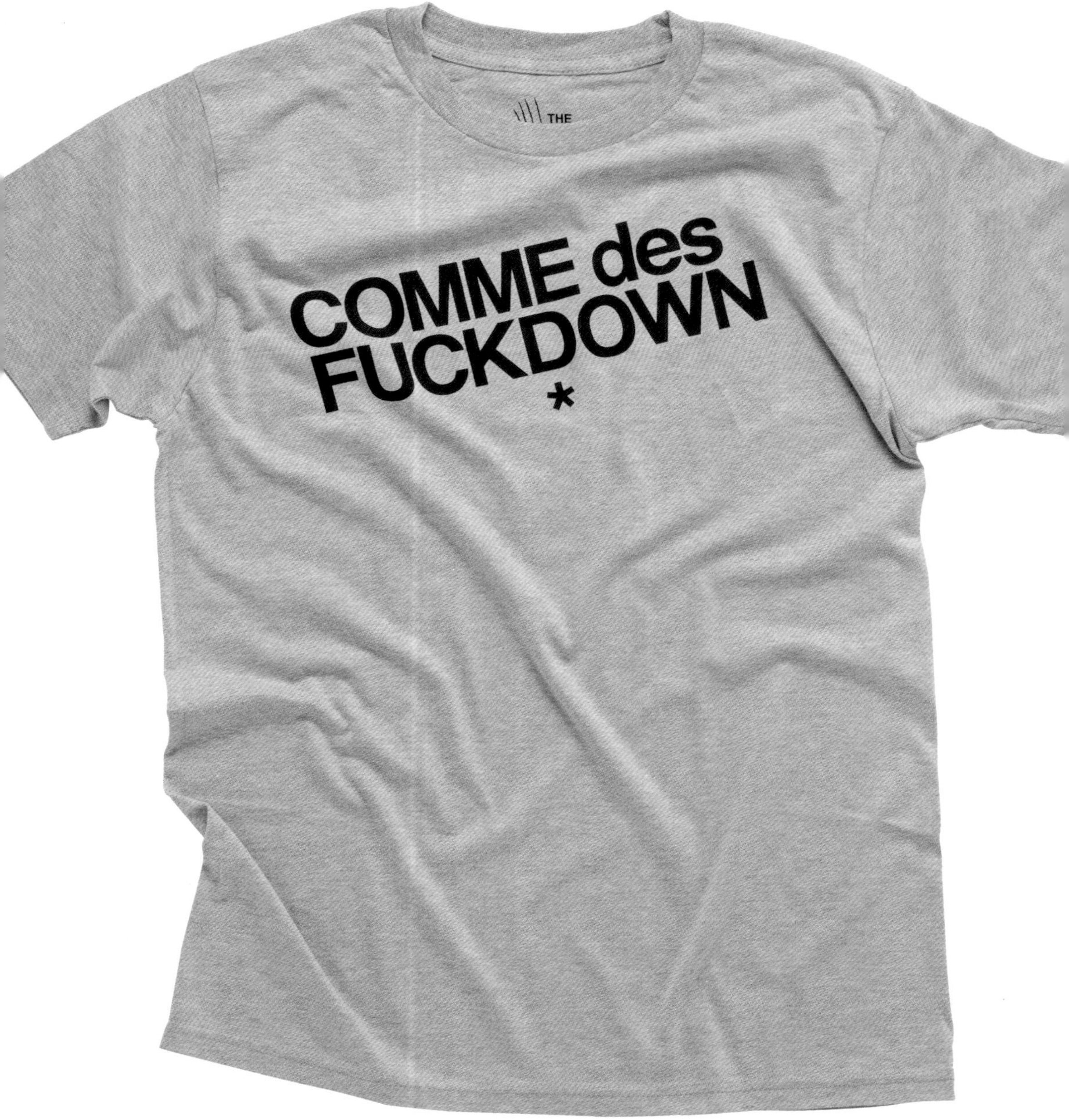
THE
COMME des
FUCKDOWN
*

This particular design started a mini revolution in streetwear graphic T-shirts when it appeared in 2012. Helped substantially by the design's association with rising Harlem rapper A$AP Rocky, the Comme design was an instant hit, becoming one of the hottest streetwear pieces almost overnight. Rocky was a figurehead for a new direction in streetwear that would borrow from high-fashion designs with an increased interest in leather and a lot of black clothing, and this piece was key to the new movement.

T-shirt designs that fit into this particular trend were strictly monochromatic, and the 'Comme des Fuckdown' design produced by The Cut, a sister label to Russ Karablin's SSUR, summed up the whole thing perfectly. The design itself is a parody of the Japanese fashion label Comme des Garçons, flipped for the streets as a graphic print and using an entirely new phrase. The designer connection and strictly monochrome colour options illustrated the streetwear-meets-high-fashion topic perfectly and it became the must-have item of that year. Though the design had first released almost a decade prior, it wasn't until 2012 that it really made a splash. Russ and his collaborators chose to bring the design back at just the right moment.

Opposite: The 'Comme des Fuckdown' design is a parody of the Japanese fashion label Comme des Garçons, flipped for the streets.

The Cut 'Comme des Fuckdown'

2012

Index

126 Mitchell Beazley would like to acknowledge and thank all those who have kindly provided material for publication in this book.

Pages 2, 10, 28, 30, 38, 46, 60, 96, 102, 106, 118 photo: Karl Adamson © Octopus Publishing Group; 8 Interim Archives/Getty Images; 12, 14, 26 Shiner.co.uk; 16, 18, 32, 34, 35, 110 courtesy STUSSY Inc.; 20, 22-23 courtesy Thrasher Magazine; 24 Ski & Sport, Unit 1, Spring Lane, Short Heath, Willenhall, West Midlands WV12 4JG; 36, 120 T-shirt kindly supplied by SSUR, photo: Karl Adamson © Octopus Publishing Group; 40, 42-43 courtesy XLARGE, photo: Robbie Jeffers; 44 The Goodhood Store, London www. goodhoodstore.com; 48 courtesy Girl Skateboards; 50 courtesy Route One Retail Limited www.routeone.co.uk ; 52 eu.bape.com; 54 courtesy Gimme 5; 56 courtesy OBEY Clothing UK www. shop.obeyclothing.co.uk; 58 acbag/ Alamy; 59 ArtAngel/Alamy; 62 courtesy Johnny Cupcakes www.johnycupcakes. com, photo: John Burke; 64 courtesy A New York Thing www.anewyorkthing. com, photo: Akira Ruiz; 66 © END; 68 top & bottom left, 69 Brand: HUF, style name: HUF x Benny Gold Etch-A-Sketch Logo Tee, colourway: black, available: hufworldwide.com; 68 bottom right Brand: HUF, style name: HUF x Benny Gold Etch-A-Sketch Skyline Tee, colourway: navy, available: hufworldwide.com; 70 Taylor Scalise; 72, 74-75 courtesy Mishka www.mishkanyc.com, photo: Sharon Marrero; 76 Kingston photography kingstonphoto.net; 78 The Social Trust; 80 DPM: Disruptive Pattern Material; 82 Staple Design; 84 Billionaire Boys Club www.bbcicecream.eu, photo: Dexter Navy; 86, 87 Billionaire Boys Club www. bbcicecream.eu; 88 courtesy Mighty Healthy www.mightyhealthy.com; 90 With permission from DTA Posse, photo: Karl Adamson © Octopus Publishing Group; 92 Bobby Hundreds; 94 T-shirt kindly supplied by Trapstar London, photo: Karl Adamson © Octopus Publishing Group; 98 With permission from Comme des Garçons, photo: Karl Adamson © Octopus Publishing Group; 100 Second Son, photo: Will Kemp; 104 Addict Clothing Company; 108 courtesy Carhartt WIP x A.P.C.; 112 With permission from Diamond Supply Co., photo: Karl Adamson © Octopus Publishing Group; 114, 116, 117 courtesy Rook www.RookBrand.com.

Acknowledgements

An Hachette UK Company
www.hachette.co.uk

First published in Great Britain in 2015
by Mitchell Beazley, a division of
Octopus Publishing Group Ltd
Carmelite House
50 Victoria Embankment
London EC4Y 0DZ
www.octopusbooks.co.uk
www.octopusbooksusa.com

Distributed in the US by
Hachette Book Group
1290 Avenue of the Americas
4th and 5th Floors
New York, NY 10020

Distributed in Canada by
Canadian Manda Group
664 Annette St.
Toronto, Ontario, Canada M6S 2C8

ISBN 978 1 84533 997 5

A CIP catalogue record for this book
is available from the British Library

Printed and bound in China

10 9 8 7 6 5 4 3 2 1

Commissioning Editor:
Joe Cottington
Editor:
Pauline Bache
Copy-editor:
Robert Anderson
Art Director:
Jonathan Christie
Design:
Untitled
Picture Researcher:
Sophie Hartley
Assistant Production Manager:
Caroline Alberti

Credits

Founded in 2009, The Daily Street is one of the world's leading destinations for up-to-date news, reviews and features on men's fashion and lifestyle, from the biggest stories in streetwear to the latest news in music, art and live events.

Based in London, the TDS team work closely with brands and retailers – from small independent start-ups to global leaders – to bring together a curated edit of happenings in the streetwear world. Whether it's exclusive interviews with key industry names, commissioned videos and photo shoots, exclusive music content or articles covering everything from classic sneakers to news on the very latest releases, The Daily Street is one of the most highly respected voices in streetwear.

www.thedailystreet.co.uk

About the author